Blue Girls

poems by

Niesha Okere

Finishing Line Press
Georgetown, Kentucky

Blue Girls

ACKNOWLEDGMENTS

Thank you to the editors and journals for publishing these poems (in earlier forms): "I'VE SEEN GOD" in Variant Literature and "Diamonds" in Allium, A Journal of Poetry & Prose.

Thank you to my parents for giving me space to tell stories, dramatics, and all. To my grandmother, for reading every word I ever put on paper. I miss you and wish I got this book out to you sooner. To my sister, thank you for being my right hand on this creative journey. To my husband, thank you for your love and unwavering support.

Thank you to Hillary Frey and Catapult for the opportunity to engage in a writing community after my 9-5.

Thank you to George W. Miller, III for affirming me and my writing after I walked into your Magazine Article Writing class many years ago.

Thank you to Finishing Line Press for helping me tell this story.

Publisher: Leah Huete de Maines
Editor: Christen Kincaid
Cover Art: Niesha Okere
Author Photo: Niesha Okere
Cover Design: Niesha Okere

Order online: www.finishinglinepress.com
also available on amazon.com

Author inquiries and mail orders:
Finishing Line Press
PO Box 1626
Georgetown, Kentucky 40324
USA

Contents

This book is dedicated to my mother.
And to all the girls I've loved before.

THERE WAS A MEETING

to plant sunflowers around the neighborhood
& nobody noticed until a sunflower pushed
a kid on their way to school. The sunflower blocked
the sidewalk, bounced side to side as it hissed
whatchu looking at?   Always late for school.

The sunflowers stand in their glory, some
as tall as light posts, course hairs,
faces wider than the sun, arms
too short to reach across
the aisle, mouths big enough
to swallow anything and anyone.

COMMON SUNFLOWER

A tall, coarse leafy plant with a hairy stem commonly branched in
the upper half and bearing several or many flower heads...

When the school bell rings, we swell
at the center of the school yard into
singular lines until flooding
security doors & metal detectors in waves
of blacks, browns, navy blues.

Contrary to common myth, the heads of sunflowers do not follow
the sun each day. However, developing flower buds and leaves do
exhibit some phototropism.

Wearing unofficial school uniforms
stained with yesterday's orange juice
black pants resurrected
from plastic bags & discount bins paired
with an empty stomach.

Sunflowers intermixed with other annuals provide good cover for
many species of wildlife. Seeds are sought by many species of wild
birds.

Running through hot hallways dressed
in long sleeves with hair grease slapped
between our thighs, book bags brushing
our knees to avoid attention.

Italicized stanzas are quotes from the University of Texas Austin's
plant database published under Helianthus annuus.

BEFORE SCHOOL MAMA SAYS

Don't be out here
Looking like a little boy   so what

Your nice shoes don't fit   my feet wide too
You get two pairs for school   what's the problem?

You cute for class   you prepared for gym
Don't worry about what other girls wear

Worry about yourself and those grades
Why ya sneakers look like that anyway?   Running ain't cute

It turns your clothes to filth
Sweats out your hair

After school I tell mama *my best*
Friend does my hair   I love   her

The feeling of fingers in my hair   the chills
Something like tiny people marching down the back of my neck

But mama don't care   she tells me
Don't let anybody play in your hair

Everybody not your friend

BEST FRIENDS

Mama said there's no such thing as best friends. Best is just another word for too close. She said the next time I think I have a best friend I need to remind myself that they're really my too close friend. Because when you let someone in they can get inside you. They know your secrets. They learn your weaknesses. And if you're sloppy enough they'll learn how you feel about them. They'll drain you. Squander your trust. They become the person you used to know.

NO NEW FRIENDS

Sometimes I like the idea of not having a best friend
it relieves the pressure
of being alone. Anticipating change
I can not control. Without
a best friend
I draft routines
preparing for solitude.

Ten minutes, two hours, an entire day,
a lifetime of living.
My idle mind no longer a weapon. I hold
my own hand creeping
through permanent records
of terrible things I did. Avoiding stamps
in red   forever alone.

My cuts no longer sing with
red lips, *she doesn't love you.*
My wedgings heal to a close
spelling   solo.

My hands rip the tips off my nails,
peel back my cuticles
until they're raw, spooling
thread from my clothes
until I unravel into sanity.

MY BEST FRIEND'S MANIFESTO

They could never be us.
    Trying to survive
        a life not worth living.

Drowning
    in desire.
They could never

be us.
    Fearing someone   will try
        to hold your hand.

They could   never
    be us.   Failing
        to suffer so your best friend can heal.

SHE DISAPPEARS

she disappears
    to places
        i cannot

            see i'm reminded
                through unanswered text messages
            that maybe

        everybody not
    your friend
these days

she doesn't
    have love
        in her eyes

            i know
                our days together
            are numbered

        soon she will
    be an empty space
beside me

WHEN SHE'S ANGRY

she cries razor sharp petals
pulled from my body
whispering words
harder than a kick
in a gut   *this is why*
                your mama don't love you
she's a cut throat
someone almost without a soul
my cut throat
my hurt soul

SOMEONE'S DIAMOND

television taught me
diamonds were a girl's best friend
so i looked to mama

i hoped she'd accept me
as her precious stone
but she already had one

shaped like a shot glass
dripping with something colorless
heavy in her hand over her lap
where my head used to go

one night i cried
so hard i dreamt
she collected my tears
one ounce at a time
to watch them spin
at the bottom of her favorite bottle

when i awoke
i wiped my tears
and poured myself
into a line of shot glasses
and left them on the kitchen table

hours later she stumbled
upon my offering
gave it a whiff
poured me back
walked away groaning about
a childlike sweetness
that wasn't strong enough
filled with a spirit distilled
one too little times

THE FIRST

I wonder what makes me the way I am. I think about ways to be different. I want to be different enough for her to love me. Maybe like me. Different enough for these cuts to not be so shallow. Like me.

They say the first cut is the deepest, but not for me. It was my most shallow, because I was shallow. I was in pain. And sometimes I can't breathe. Or see. Other me sits on the ceiling watching anxious me undo myself in between jam sessions where I forget who I am.

I'VE SEEN GOD

They stood in mama's kitchen. She called
to them as she struggled to open a box of hair dye.
God dipped her painted head under a running faucet
as she prayed for hair darker & shinier than daddy's
shoes on a Sunday morning.

Mama caught her reflection on a rusty kettle before
snatching that pink hand mirror from the kitchen table
& screamed Damn grays!   Excuse me, Lord. What a miracle
'cause I didn't know God made house calls.

I've only seen God in the tight aisles of beauty
supply stores to assist people near those spin displays
that hold mama's beloved wet & wild lipsticks
that used to cost one dollar. God pops in & out
to settle customer disputes one Oh, Lord, $1.29? at a time,
never lingering for more than a few seconds. I didn't see

God myself. I saw them through mama's eyes. Her tears
played back the days long hair draped her back. She hummed
about her pick of men lined up around the corner just
to get a whiff. She drove her own car. Made
her own money.

I heard God lift her voice to sing about the pressure steeping
from inside. Mama danced in my face to the sound of her hair
breaking towards the linoleum floors one strand at a time. I watched
the longest strand migrate to a soft space she was told
to make room for   me.

She sobbed as everything beautiful washed down the drain until
it was just   me.

SOME GIRLS TURN BLUE

staring at the sky
afraid to catch their breath, collecting
tears in old jars never emptying
them

distracting themselves with shards
of found glass used to halve hearts
while in search of
someone less

thoughts shifting between worlds, heads
rising & falling with the sun, never looking
in familiar places

THE DAY I MET MY BEST FRIEND

she wore a diamond studded headband that matched my sneakers.
She yelled at me. Her eyes locked on my feet   *why you wearing
purple?* Her eyebrows crumbled. Hair wet from the rain. Purple
stains on her white shirt. Body reeking of something from my
mama's kitchen. Something blue with magic mixed with ammonia.
Maybe pancake syrup.

SHE SHOWS HER LEGS

when it's too warm for stockings
that run from her knees   she stops
wearing love on her wrist   she stops
wearing hair down her back made from synthetic
strands banded & torn from dusty packages pulled
from tiny aisles at the hair store   she stops
forcing sleeves over her hands & learns
to be happy like when we sit at the end
of lunch tables eating hot slices of good pizza
with cheese that stretches for miles & tiny
pepperonis that curl at the ends pulled
from plastic bags & cooked in metal
ovens paid for with borrowed lunch tickets

MY MANIFESTO

Make her feel loved.
Make her feel loved.
Make her feel loved.
Make her feel loved.
Make her feel loved.
Make her feel loved.
Make her feel loved.
Make her feel loved.
Make her feel loved.
Make her feel loved.
Make her feel loved.
Make her feel loved.
Make her feel loved.
Make her feel loved.
Make her feel loved.
Make her feel loved.
Make her feel loved.
Make her feel loved.
Make her feel loved.
Make her feel loved.
Make her feel loved.

Make her feel loved.

WHEN SHE DISAPPEARS I WONDER

where broken hearts go
& how to get her's back
cause i want to love her

when she disappears
i wonder how to cast spells
to undead her love

i summon pieces of her broken heart
to stop the darkness from coming
between us
cause i text really long messages

when she disappears
i bite my tongue
swallow what's left
awaiting her reply

i remember her secrets
refusing to swallow them

when she disappears
i tend to our toothless garden
refusing her
the desire to die
alone

I TOLD HER

my first cut was shallow
because I worship a god
of beauty

I told her how
I hold my breath & close
my eyes
pulling and folding
small pieces of myself
arguing with old wounds
about order of importance

I told her I feared death
because   what if
it isn't pretty   what if
people won't notice   what if
it's not that deep

CITY BLUES

I heard blue is the color of water.

That makes me laugh.
I want to move away.

Cause it's nothing like the water I know.
In a city where I want to drown and pull myself out.

I stand over the concrete ledge
along the city's waterworks to dream

of cold brown water chewing my pain
& collecting my blues in its teeth.

As I swallow the sunlight and sediment flooding
my city. I can make it

beautiful around here. The battle of flesh, black
& blue in my chest as I rise above

the tall buildings that crowd my neighborhood.
Sending a message to everyone I love.

WHEN WE'RE TOGETHER

our mouths open
towards the sky, swaying
in the breeze, singing
songs as we're engulfed
by the sun. drying out, awaiting
someone to chop us into nothing
for our seedlings to grow

we need a breakthrough

Niesha Okere is a writer, poet, and multimedia storyteller from Philadelphia. Her work has appeared in *Variant Literature, Allium, A Journal of Poetry & Prose, hex,* and elsewhere. Niesha received her B.A. in Journalism from Temple University.

www.ingramcontent.com/pod-product-compliance
Lightning Source LLC
Chambersburg PA
CBHW022108080426
42734CB00009B/1519